WITOLD LUTOSLAWSKI

Album for the Young

FOLK MELODIES (1945)

BUCOLICS (1952)

PIECES FOR THE YOUNG (1953)

INVENTION (1968)

AN OVERHEARD TUNE (1957)

Exclusive Distributors:
Music Sales Limited
8/9 Frith Street, London W1V 5TZ.

This book © Copyright 1991 by Chester Music Limited
Order No. CH59287
ISBN 0.7119.2529.1

Art Direction by Michael Bell Design.
Cover illustration by Lara Harwood.
Typesetting by Capital Setters.

Chester Music Limited
(A division of Music Sales Limited)

1. Oh, My Johnny

Oh, mon Jeannot
Ach, mein Hanschen

Witold Lutoslawski (1945)

2

Sostenuto ♪=ca 126

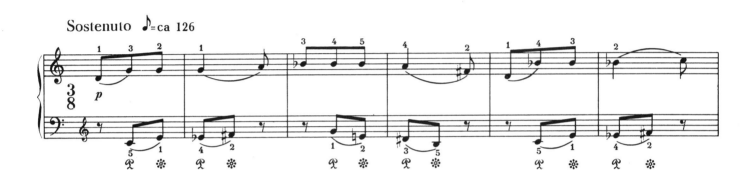

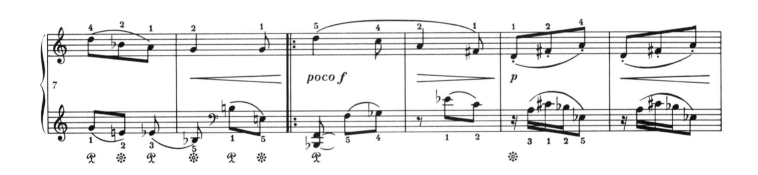

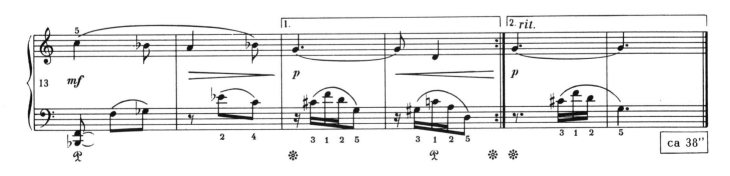

ca 38''

2. Hey, I Come From Cracow

He! c'est de Cracovie que je viens
Heda! ich komme von Krakau

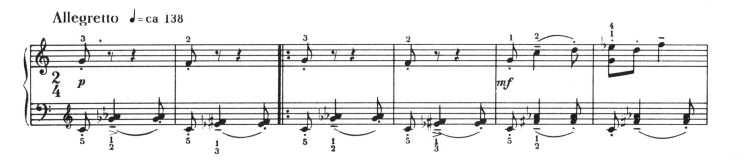

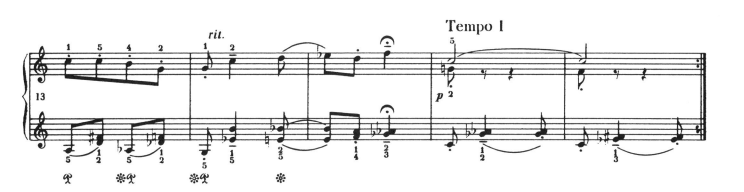

ca 35''

3. There Is A Path, There Is

Il y a un petit sentier
Es gibt einen kleinen Weg

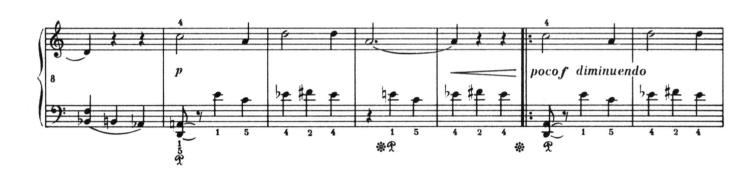

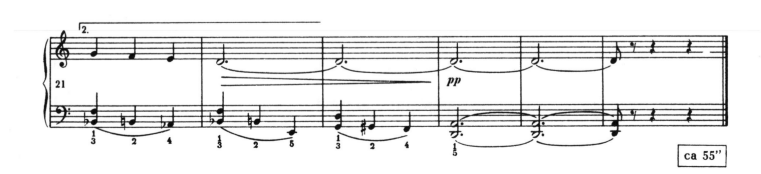

ca 55''

4. The Shepherd Girl

La petite bergère
Das Hirtenmädchen

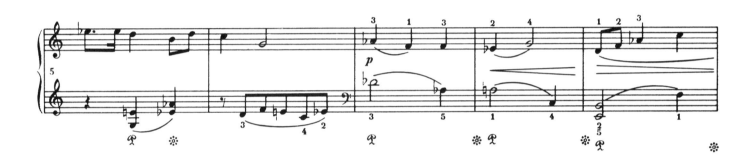

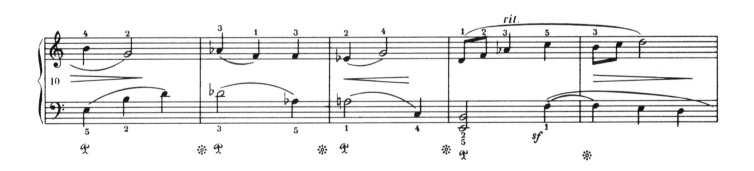

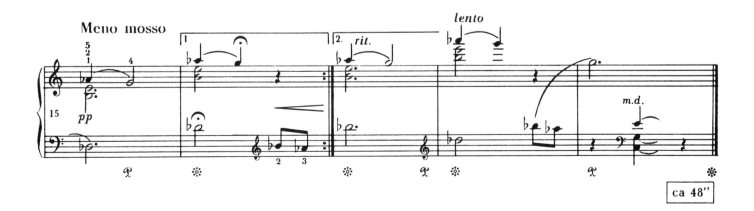

ca 48''

5. An Apple Hangs On The Apple-tree

Une pomme sur le pommier
Hängt ein Apfel am Apfelbaum

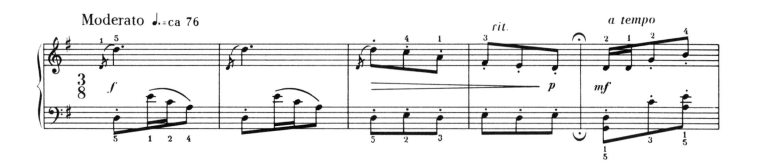

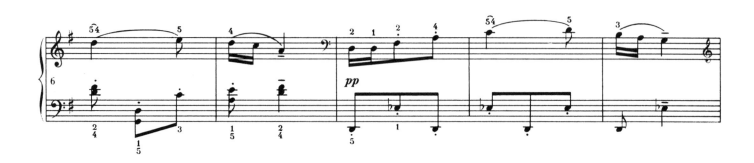

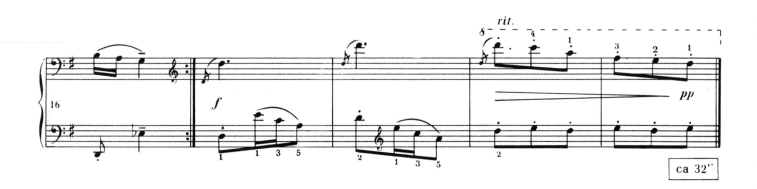

ca 32''

6. A River Flows From Sieradz

Une rivière vient de Sieradz
Von Sieradz fließt ein Fluß

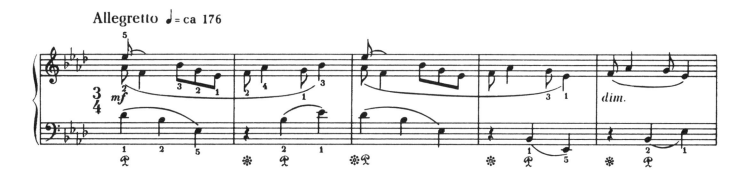

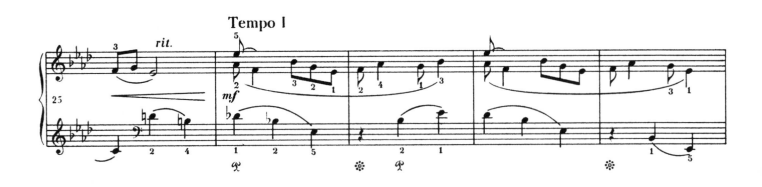

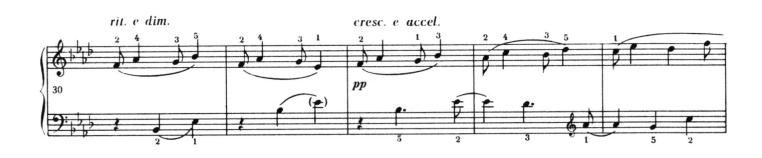

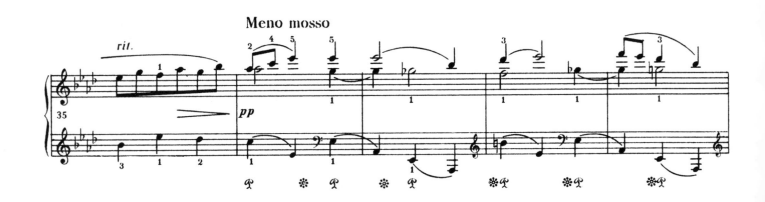

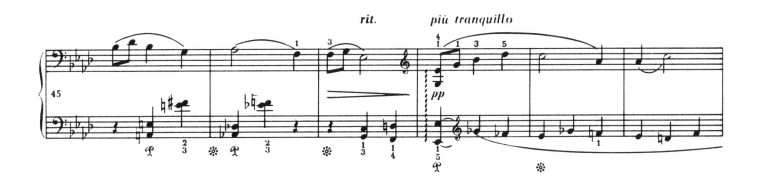

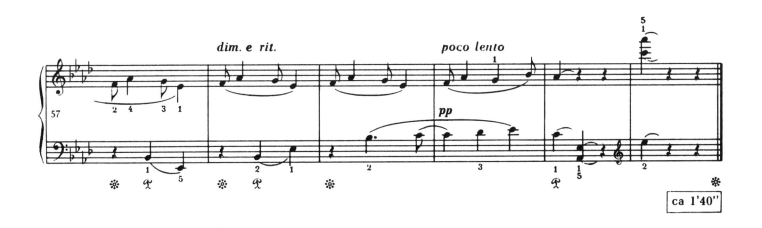

ca 1'40''

7. Master Michael

Compère Michel
Herr Michael

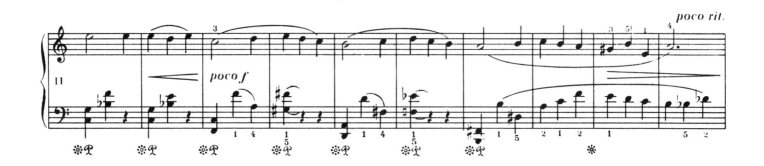

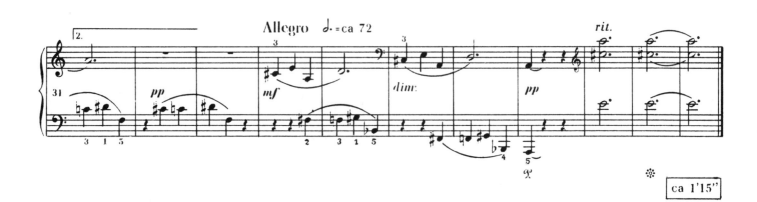

ca 1'15''

8. The Lime-tree In The Field

Le tilleul dans le champ
In Feld ein Lindenbäumchen

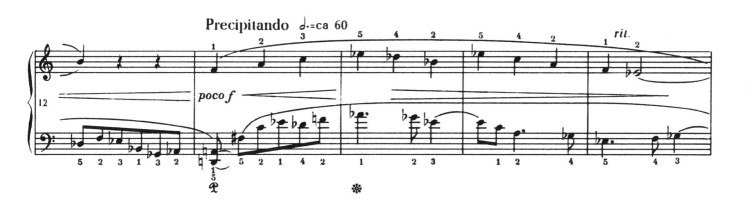

ca 50"

9. Flirting

Coquette
Flirtaud/kokett

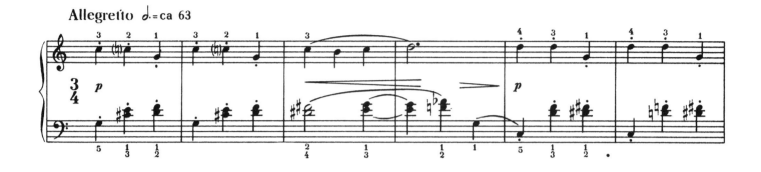

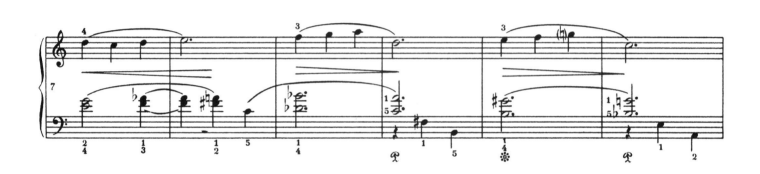

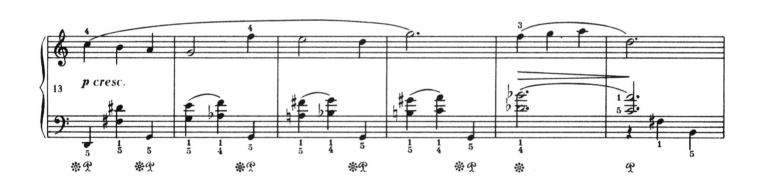

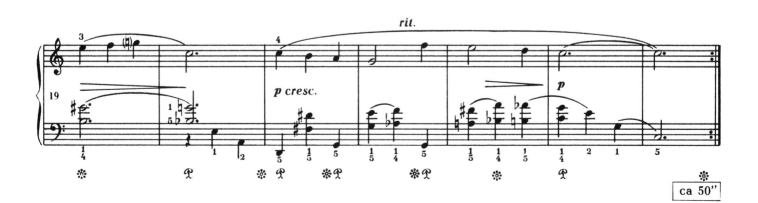

ca 50"

10. The Grove

La bosquet
Der Hain

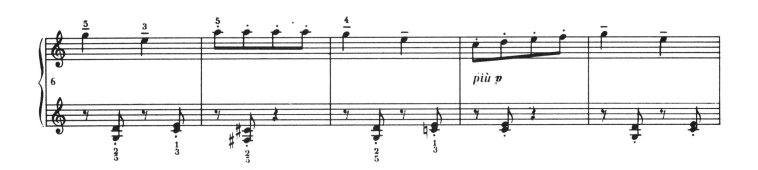

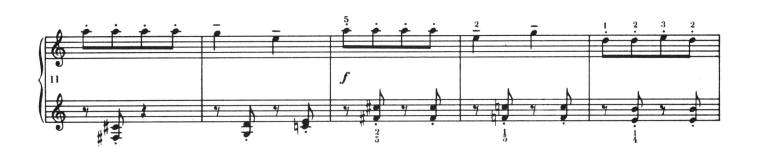

14

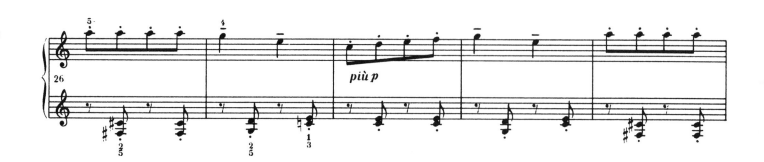

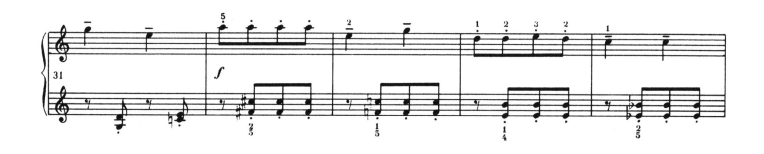

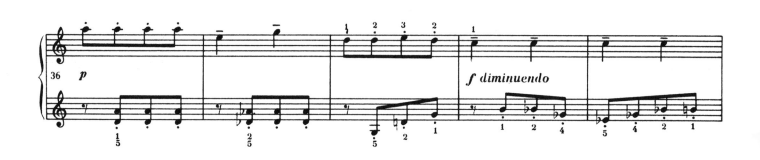

ca 30''

11. The Gander

Le jars
Der Gänserich

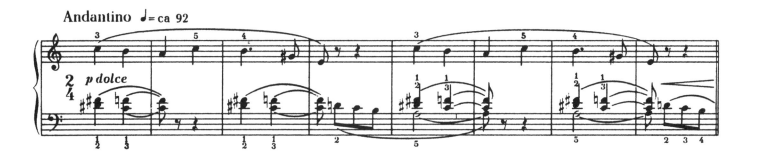

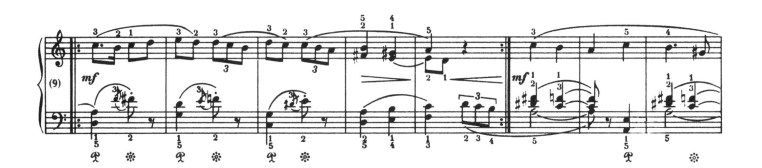

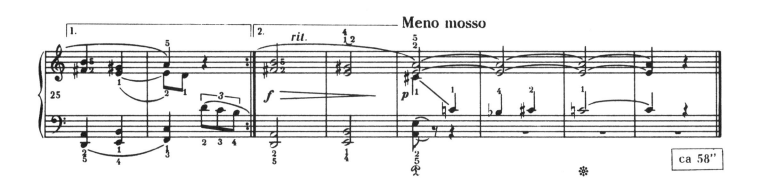

ca 58''

12. *The Schoolmaster*

Le recteur
Der Rektor

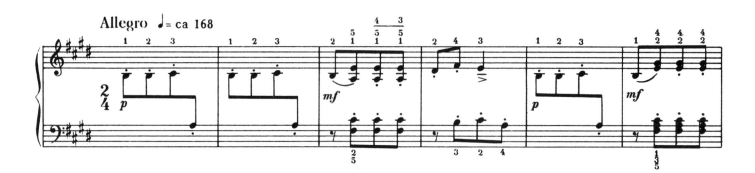

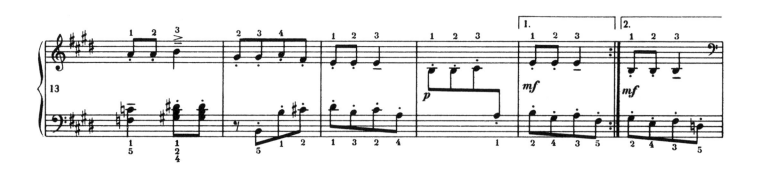

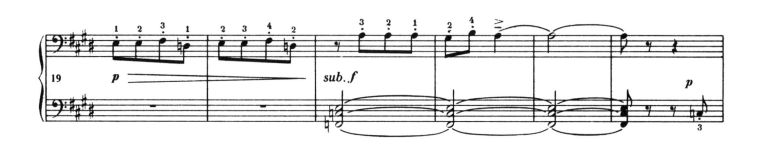

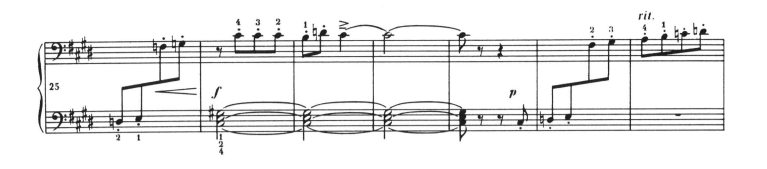

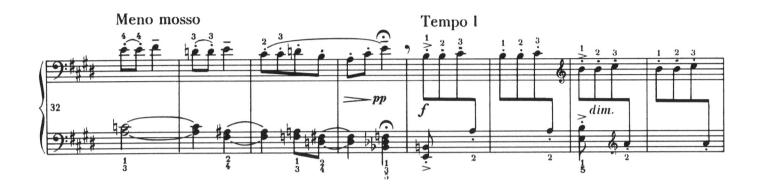

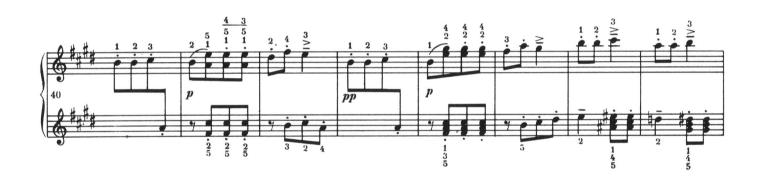

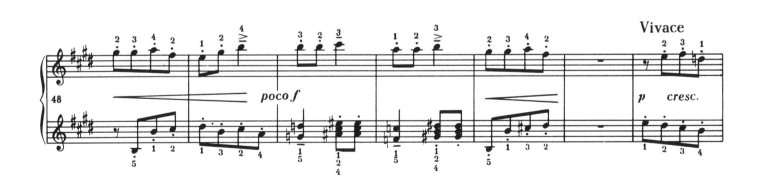

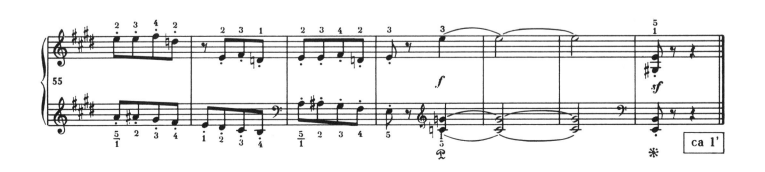

BUCOLICS
BUCOLIQUES
5 BUKOLIKA

Witold Lutoslawski (1952)

poco sostenuto

Tempo I

rit.

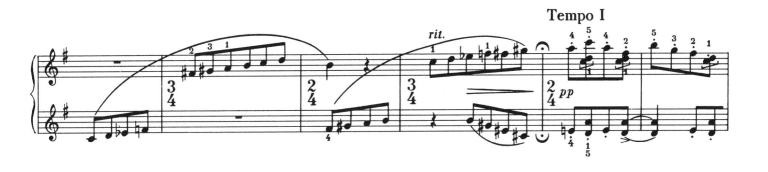

cresc.

Tempo I

poco accelerando

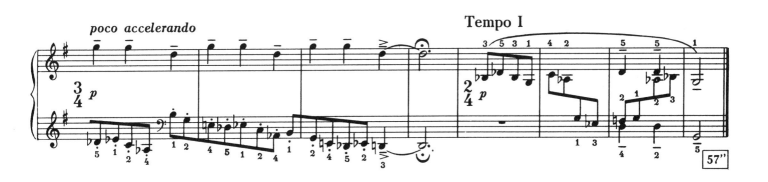

57"

2

20

3

Allegro molto ♩.=104

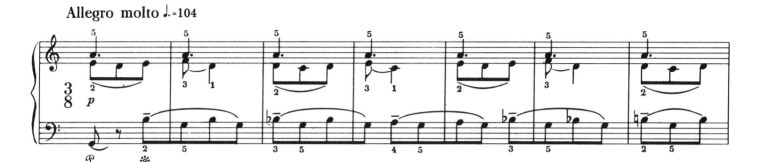

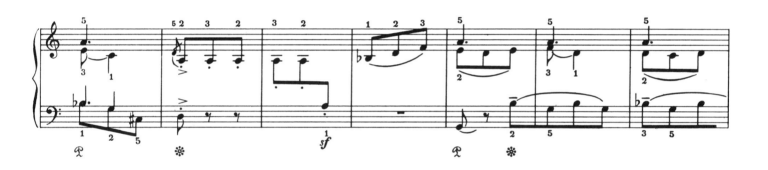

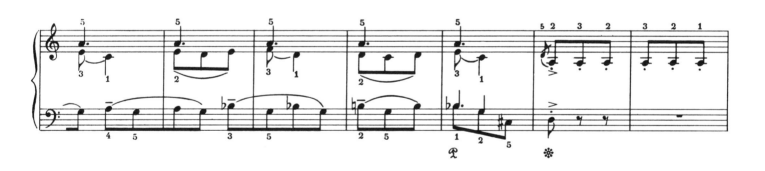

poco f

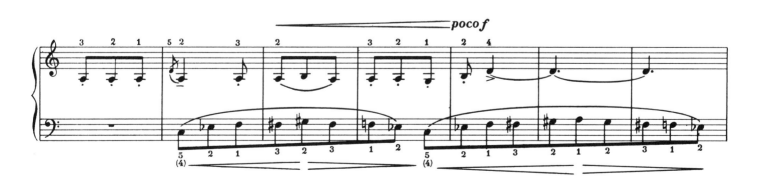

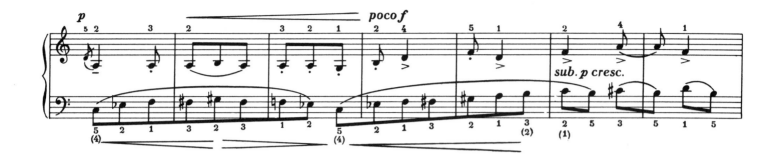

22

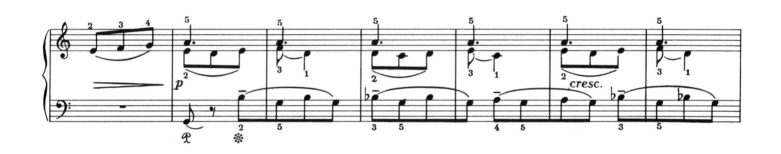

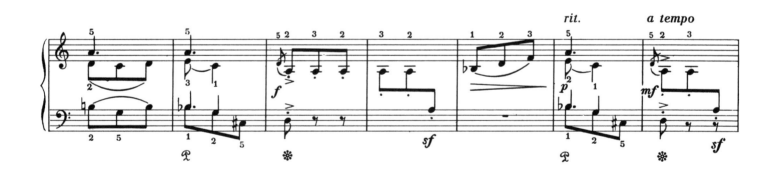

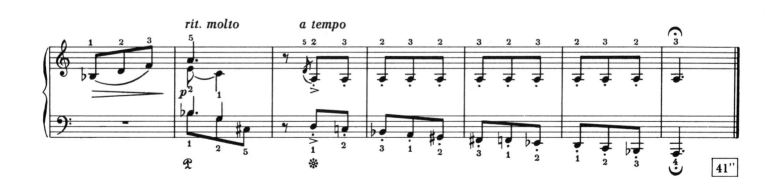

41"

4

1'28"

5

Allegro marciale ♩=184

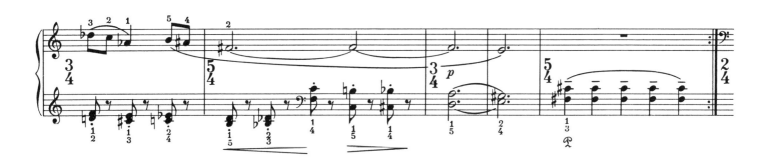

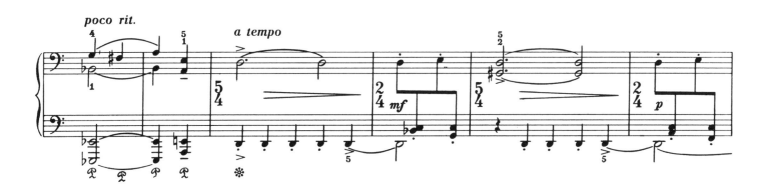

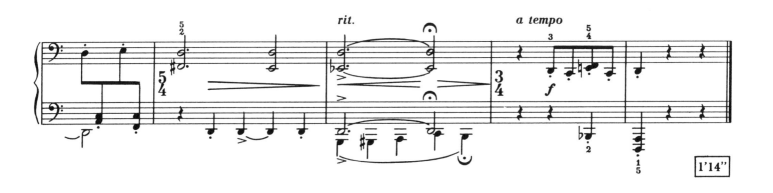

1'14"

3 PIECES FOR THE YOUNG

3 PIÈCES POUR LES JEUNES
3 STÜCKE FÜR DIE JUGEND

Witold Lutoslawski (1953)

1. Four-Finger Exercise

Etude à quatre doigts
Vierfingerübung

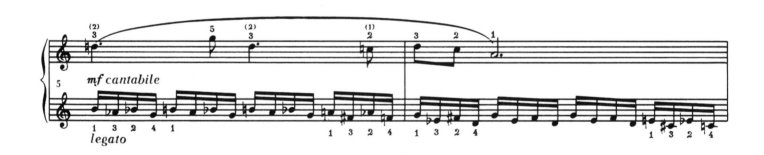

ca 54''

2. An Air

Une mélodie
Melodie

Andante con moto ♩=ca 60

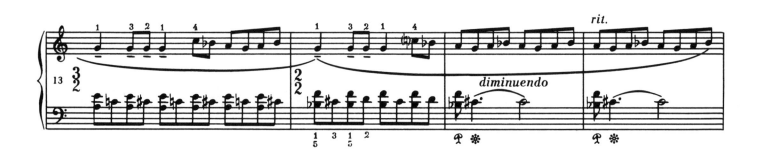

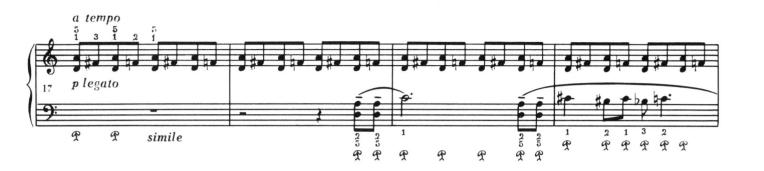

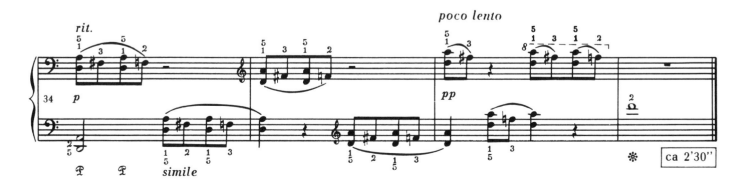

3. March

La Marche
Marsch

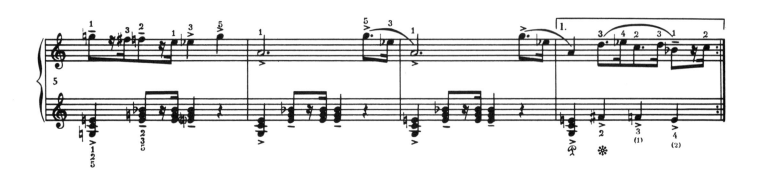

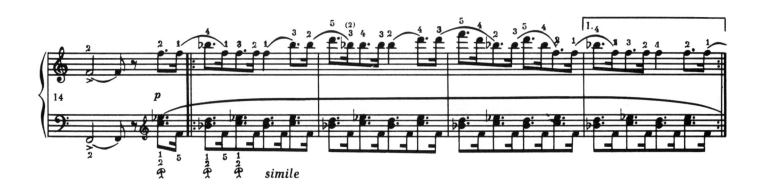

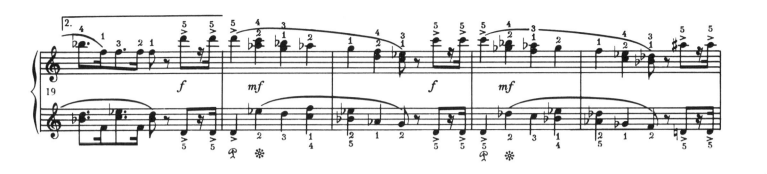

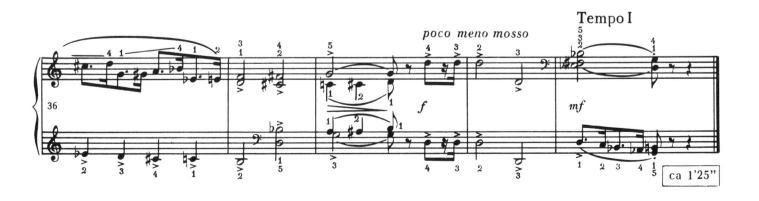

INVENTION
UNE INVENTION
INVENTION

Witold Lutoslawski (1968)

32

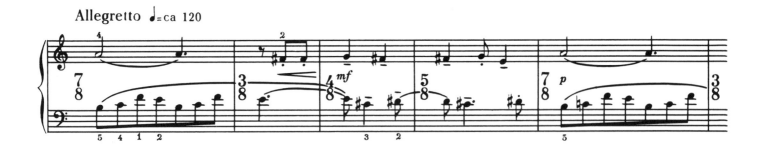

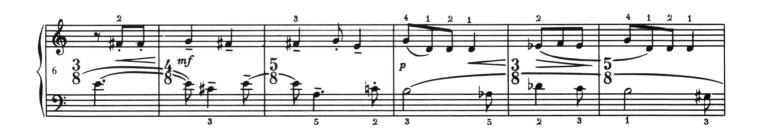

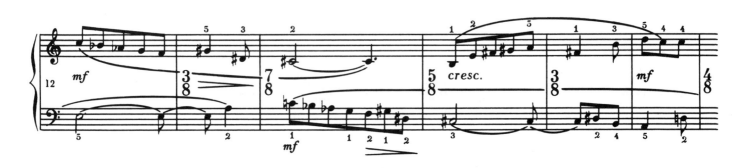

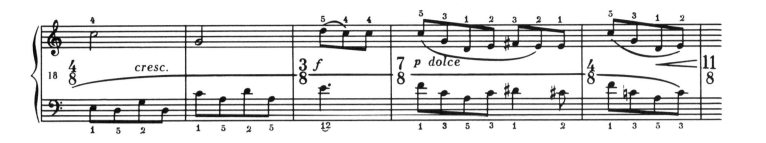

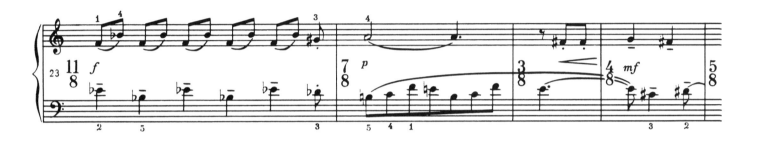

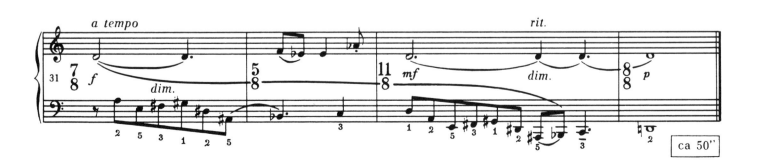

ca 50''

AN OVERHEARD TUNE
SOUVENIR D'UNE MÉLODIE
DIE ZUFÄLLIG GEHÖRTE MELODIE

Witold Lutoslawski (1957)

Tempo di marcia. Veloce

34

7

14

38

Printed in England by Caligraving Limited Thetford Norfolk

5/96 (26169)

WITOLD LUTOSLAWSKI
Album for the Young

Performance Notes:

In the difficult climate of post-war Poland, Lutoslawski found it necessary to pursue two parallel strands of compositional activity. The work which he regards as 'serious' concentrated on his First Symphony, begun in Warsaw during the Nazi occupation and completed in 1947.

Meanwhile, he supported himself and his family by writing what he calls 'functional' music, including a vast quantity of incidental music for the theatre, film scores, songs, and simple pieces based on folk material.

Immediately after the war there was not yet any official requirement for composers in Poland to write according to the Stalinist principles of socialist-realism; that came later. Thus when Lutoslawski embarked upon his earliest folk-based pieces, he was returning to plans made before the war, rather than responding to any sinister political influences.

If politics are to be taken as a background for understanding the use of folk material in the brief post-war honeymoon period (before the establishment of a Soviet-style socialist state in 1947), it should be remembered that all manifestations of Polish national culture had been suppressed during the Nazi occupation (including the music of Chopin).

Under these circumstances, it is only natural that there was a spontaneous and entirely sincere affirmation of national identity expressed in many ways, including music.

Lutoslawski's set of twelve Folk Melodies for piano (1945) was written in response to a commission from the newly founded state music publishing house based in Cracow, PWM. Unlike Bartók, whose folk materials were gathered through his own ethno-ecological musical research, Lutoslawski drew upon tunes gathered by others, in this case a collection by Jerzy Olszewski.

The first public performance of the set was given in Cracow by Zbigniew Drzewiecki in 1946. The real significance of these pieces, however, was confirmed by their adoption as prescribed teaching materials for Poland's specialist music schools.

Separate regulations of 1958, 1959 and 1961 issued by the Ministry of Culture ensured that successive generations of young Polish musicians would study and play Lutoslawski's Folk Melodies as part of their syllabus.

The twelve pieces represent several different parts of Poland. No.1 uses a tune from Lowicz in the western region of Mazovia. As the title of No.2 makes explicit, its tune is from the ancient capital, Cracow. Nos.3 and 4 use melodies from the Podlasie region due east of the modern capital, Warsaw. The tunes of Nos.5 and 6 both originate from the town and area of Sieradz in 'Great Poland' (Wielko Polska); hence the title of the sixth piece refers specifically to the river Warta, which continues its journey to Poznan and later forms a tributary of the Oder.

The origin of No.7 is of particular significance to Lutoslawski's own background. It is a waltz from the mostly forested Kurpie region, an area north-west of Warsaw defined by the river Narew and its various tributaries.

Although born in Warsaw, the composer spent much of his childhood in that region, on the family estates at Drozdowo. No.8 uses a tune from the Mazurian lake district in the north-east of Poland, bordering on the territories of East Prussia which now find themselves in the Soviet Union. Mazuria has given us the Mazurka, but the piece in question uses a melody typical of the region rather than the more famous dance form. The last four pieces are all dances from Silesia.

The set of five Bucolics (1952), commissioned by PWM, also uses tunes from the Kurpie region, this time drawn from a collection by Father Wladyslaw Skierkowski. The first performance was given in Warsaw by the composer himself in December 1953. One of the most interesting aspects of the Bucolics is the way they demonstrate Lutoslawski's predilection for polymetric effects.

This principle of superimposing different metres (whether with changes of time signature or not), is also much in evidence in the Dance Preludes for clarinet and piano of 1954. The composer also arranged the Bucolics for viola and cello in 1962, although this version was not publicly performed or published until 1973.

The Three Pieces for Young People were commissioned by PWM in 1953. In technical terms the first may be a four-finger exercise, but in compositional terms it is an exercise in the use of interlocking major and minor thirds. It is also a kind of simple study in perpetual semiquaver motion.

The second piece makes use of a triadic ostinato pattern which oscillates continually between major and minor. The final piece of the set is a March which makes more than a passing glance in the direction of Prokofiev.

The little two-part Invention is a 'pièce d'occasion' written in 1968 to celebrate the 71st birthday of Stefan Śledziński. Lutoslawski has produced a number of such miniatures for specific occasions over the years, but they should not be counted with the functional pieces or equated with the folk orientation of their stylistic approach.

An Overheard Tune is one of Lutoslawski's last folk-based pieces. Although repeated many times, the tune does not really develop. Instead, the composer enlivens the piece by introducing some bi-tonal passages, in which the two players each read from a different key signature at the same time. This leads to one player using the white keys whilst the other uses the black ones. Thus Lutoslawski achieves a relatively sophisticated musical effect even though the individual parts are kept quite simple.

Written for and dedicated to Zosia Owińska, An Overheard Tune dates from 1957, the same year that Lutoslawski made the decisive step into the new harmonic language which he had been painstakingly evolving during the years of Stalinist control. The first work to employ his new harmonic language, the Five Songs to poems of Kazimiera Illakowicz, drew a clear line in his career.

After this point he would never again return to composition based on folk materials, except for some arrangements of his earlier work. A highly productive chapter in Lutoslawski's life had closed. But a much more exciting one was only just beginning.

Charles Bodman Rae – Ilkley 1991